The Road To World War 3

Can the Dark forces of anti-Freedom trump Humanity?

How to use the Book:

1) The book is divided into 3 Sections. Every Section is a stage in the Drama. Sections have 7 chapters. With 1, 2 & 4 chapters for Sections I, II & III respectively.

2) Each chapter is titled according to the pivotal event it is triggered by. Note that a particular chapter contains much more than what the title suggests. For example, in Chapter 4, Osama Bin Laden's rise is the start to a series of events which lead us to more clues. But the title denotes only the first event in the long series, that is Laden's rise.

3) Read the book sequentially for better impact and understanding. That way, the reader will be able to connect the dots in the complex drama more easily and lucidly. Read at least one Section in one sitting. It will help the reader register events and trends more easily.

4) This book does not predict the future, nor does the author claim to have inside information on the happening of the world. It is a scientific study of events. It is analysis.

5) Lastly, read this book as a grand drama unfolding before our eyes. It is fascinating and scary at the same time.

Table of Contents

Preface

Photo: Getty Images / Yavuz Alatan.

Dec. 20, 2016. A Turkish policeman, who used to provide security to Turkey's President, shoots down the Russian ambassador in Ankara. An obvious provocation. Putin for the last many months has been pounding ISIS strongholds in Syria. ISIS, a creation of Sunni Saudi Arabia to keep a check on Shia Iran, is also supported covertly by Turkey, U.S. and Israel. The Jabhat Fateh al-Sham organization (formerly the al-Nusra Front) claims responsibility. The Syria-based terror group puts out a statement: **"...the assassination of the Russian ambassador was the "first act of revenge" for the women, children and the elderly killed in Aleppo as well as all the Muslims killed across the world."**

New York Daily, instead of condemning the act of terror, justifies the killing of the Russian ambassador "because he worked for Putin". Imagine the outrage if it was the ambassador of an US ally! This is the level of polarisation we are experiencing.

Just hours after the tragedy, a Pakistan-born refugee, who arrived in Germany this February, rams a truck into a busy Berlin Christmas market. More than 12 dead, 48 injured.

Pic courtesy: Getty Images.

Events such as these are increasingly becoming a part of our daily lives. So frequent are these tragedies that London's first Muslim Mayor shamelessly claimed, "Terror attacks are "part and parcel of life in a big city".

Nov. 8, 2016. Donald J. Trump is elected the 45th President of the United States after a relentless campaign characteristized by populism, hatred for the mainstream media and a fear of the future of White America. Initially ridiculed as a joke, he galvanised millions of voters to vote for him. This, just months after Brexit, an event that left Western Europe shattered. No one expected these events to happen, but they did.

All this can only mean one thing; there is something far greater at work, something which is not spelled out openly in public, for fear of backlash or panic or some other political reason"; that politicians are not telling us the truth. It is said that the analysis of war can't be done openly in public. But isn't it true that the consequences of war are borne by the very same public, while political leaders retreat to their "safe zones", guarded by heavily armed men, funded by taxpayers!

The purpose of this book is not just to document the events which have happened in the past. It's a study of what might come in the future. How the various characters in this drama and their geopolitical interests collide or combine to shape the world of tomorrow.

The beacon of Democracy is slowly drowning in the sea of blood, hatred and greed. Even the so-called democratic nations have started moving away from its values and ideals. India, the world's largest democracy is riddled with corruption and nepotism. Add to this the constant threat of war from all sides. Britain, the mother of parliamentary system, is riddled with similar issues of corruption and inaction. Germany is committing collective suicide by allowing millions of unchecked refugees to come in and change its demographic. America may seem to be relatively stable, but populism, debt-fueled growth, corporatism and drugs are wreaking havoc silently.

In the time to come, the situation will be exponentially more messy. And while big shifts can be better analysed by "connecting the dots", it is always good to know where we are headed rather than be clueless about the future. Hence this work...

Introduction:

Trump. Putin. Brexit. Syria.
Are we living through the run-up to the Third World War? Is there a method to this madness raging all around us? What if this is just the last part of a Trilogy, a series that started some 100 years ago? And what will happen next? These are some of questions the book seeks to answer.

Trump was not supposed to win. Brexit was not supposed to happen. Islamist Jihad was supposed to die when Osama Bin Laden was dispatched to hell. And the 2008 crisis-driven bail-outs were supposed to solve our economic problems. Everything that was supposed to happen, did not happen. And not only did it not happen, actually the opposite took place!

We are living in a world with plenty of "black swans". A Black Swan is a creature that is rare. An event so unlikely, yet looking back it makes perfect sense. Wonder why we believed it won't occur?! This book attempts to inform the reader of the black swans of the past so that he or she spots those rare creatures in the future!

Starting from a brief background on World Wars 1 & 2, the book quickly gets into the thick of things. Things like the phenomenal rise of Islamist Jihad in the past 20 years, the stunning economic "de-leveraging" of the Western world, and the spectacular rise of China. The book seeks to tie it all in together, so that the reader makes sense of what is happening around. A world that seems complex and unpredictable begins to look more sequential and clear as the analysis dives deeper into events: past & present. Finally, the book tries to connect the dots looking back; to paint a picture that is still unclear. A picture of the future. Of all the characters and their motivations factored in. What emerges is a scary, yet somewhat hopeful situation. A world in transition.

Third World War is the reality we are living through, which can be described by the phrase, "The Perfect Storm". It is a military conflict on a global scale and at different levels. It has many dimensions like Economic, Social, Religious, Geopolitical and Ideological. The three trends shaping

WW3 are: 1) The rise of Jihad in the middle-east & beyond; 2) China's military expansion & modernization; 3) The economic de-leveraging of the western world.

The above 3 trends could be approximately mapped on a timeline in phases as follows:
1) 2014-2018 (Incremental or rising violence phase)
2) 2018-2019 (Peak violence phase)
3) 2019-2025 (Decremental or rehabilitation phase)

The above 3 phases are characterized by the combined strength of the 3 trends noted earlier above. Meaning from 2014 to 2018-19, global violence will keep rising owing to all 3 trends gaining momentum. In this phase, Islamist Jihad will continue gaining strength. Partly because the West refuses to act against it due to political correctness, and partly because of Jihad owns inherent devilish characteristics. Phase-I will also witness Western world's continued de-leveraging (a downward economic spiral fueled by excessive debt. Combine this with China's rising military muscle.

Phase-2 is the consequence of Phase-1. An emboldened Jihad machine grows more audacious. A debt-laden Western world fights to survive, while an aggressive China decides to double down! Violence knows no bounds, as even the pretense of ethics, decency and basic human dignity are thrown out of the window. All masks are off. Pure quantitative power is the norm as the Third World War goes through its peak!

Then something unbelievable happens. Phase-3 is full of surprises. Equations which are taken for granted suddenly seem shaky. The Devil no longer has any tricks left up its sleeve. The free world grapples for breath, but is still alive. For the first time in this War, evil's victory and freedom's defeat are not a given. What will happen. How it will happen. And who will be the Hero.

Read on dear readers...

SECTION I

Chapter 1: The Beginning.
When a small spark starts a wildfire.

Pic courtesy: Diercke International Atlas.

Europe before WW1.

28 June, 1914. **Archduke Franz Ferdinand** of **Austria**, heir presumptive to the **Austro-Hungarian** throne, and his wife Sophie, Duchess of Hohenberg, were shot dead by Gavrilo Princip and other Austrians of the Slav origin in Sarajevo. The political objective of the assassination was to break off Austria-Hungary's **South Slav** provinces so they could be combined into a Yugoslavia.

In those days, only France and Switzerland were Republics. In Great Britain, although the Parliament did exist alongside the Monarchy, its attitude was that of a feudal lord out to swallow the entire world. Already the largest empire on earth, its power was hugely disproportionate to its tiny size.

Russia was ruled by The House of **Romanov. All other nations were ruled by dynasties who cherished the goal of building an empire as large or even greater than that of Great Britain. It was competitive colonialism at its peak.**

Each empire spied on the other and felt insecure about other's plans on the geopolitical chessboard. They did undertake friendship treaties and pacts, but it was a smokescreen. What was beneath the pretense wa deep hatred, jealousy and greed to conquer more territory and power.

At the time, there were two groups of nations pitted against each other. On one hand were Britain, France and Russia, forming the Triple Entente. Opposing group was comprised of Germany, Austria-Hungary and Italy forming the Triple Alliance. As these nations came to each other's aid after the assassination, their war declarations produced a domino effect.

On July 28, 1914 Austria-Hungary declared war on Serbia.
On August 2, Germany signs a secret pact with the Ottoman Empire.

Russia, which had fought a war with Imperial Japan, and had to retreat shamefully, wanted to prove its strength, not just to the world but also to the demoralized people of Russia. Japan, a speck in comparison to the geographic giant Russia, had turned an upset on the Bear. To restore the pride of the Russian people, a war between Austria and Serbia was a golden opportunity.

Russians declared that the Slav origin peoples of Serbia are actually Russian in ethnicity and declared a war on Austria. Russia began massive military recruitment, which also did the job of lowering domestic unemployment rate. The dual purpose of restoring pride and deflecting an inherent revolt was achieved.

Kaiser, the German monarch believed, and so did the common German, that Germany and Austria are bound by the love of their native land. That they were the same people. Kaiser saw this war as a chance to expand Germany's territory and declared a war on the enemies of Austria.

As Germany started planned attacks on Serbia, France became restless. Other nations had always feared the well-equipped German war machine. Soon Great Britain joined France is declaring war on Germany.

And so it came to be. A small war between two tiny states, started because of an assassination, took the form of a world war! Great Britain, France and Russia fighting against Germany...

The First Battle of Ypres.

Ypres, in western Belgium. The first terrible battle fought between Germany and Great Britain/France was at Ypres, a strategically important place. As the German Army advanced toward the English channel, British forces fought hard. German, French and Belgian armies and the British Expeditionary Force (BEF) fought from Arras in France to Neiuport on the Belgian coast, from 10 October to mid-November. 134,315 German casualties in Belgium and northern France!

Pic courtesy: The Great War Project.

The most significant part of this battle was this Hitler and his associate, Hess, were among the survivors! As ordinary soldiers, their experience in this battle would go on to trigger many novel, and cruel, ideas in Hitler's mind.

Battle of the Somme.

Between July 1 and November 18, 1916, the armies of British and french empires fought an intense battle with the Germans on both sides of the upper reaches of river Somme in France. The massive casualties resulting from the battle sent shockwaves of anger and despair across Great Britain. The nation lost more than 420,000 soldiers in that single battle.

Pic courtesy: The Sun newspaper, News Corp.

The rage across Great britain was so great that its government fell. A new ministry was formed by the consensus of all political parties, and a new minister for arms supplies was appointed. That man was Winston Churchill.

All along Germany had suffered massive casualties of its own. 500,000 in Somme itself! By November 1918, Germany was defeated on all fronts. Kaiser, the German monarch fled the country. The sun had set on the German royal family.

Victory of Great Britain and France in this war was primarily due to the fact that they had used toxic gases against german soldiers at many places. The same toxic gas Hitler used during the Second World War against Jews. It made Hitler to go blind temporarily during the First World War. It was at that time when he vowed to avenge the act and give his enemies a strong of dose of their own medicine.

Europe after the War:

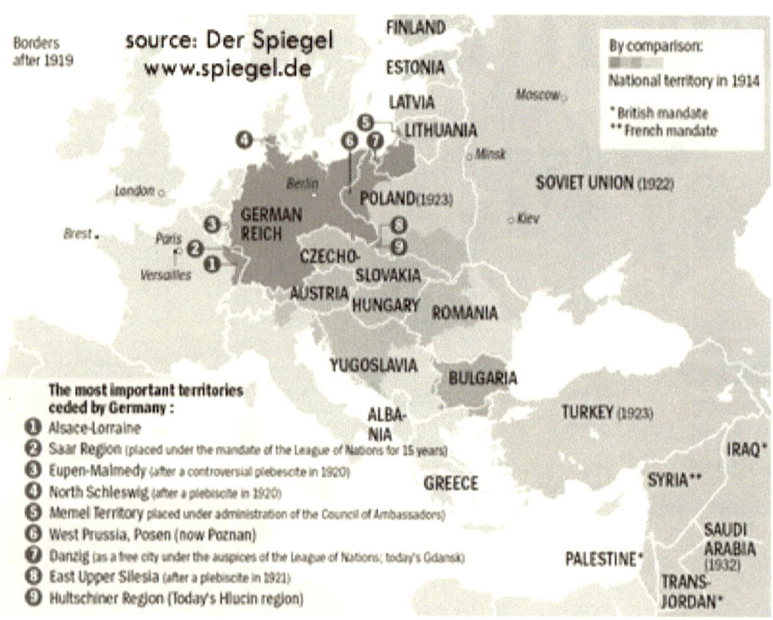

Pic courtesy: Der Spiegel.

Germany became a Republic after its defeat.

The Treaty of Versailles.

On 28 June 1919, exactly five years after the assassination of Archduke Franz Ferdinand, a peace treaty was signed between the now defeated Germany and the victorious Allied Powers. Of the many provisions in the treaty, one of the most important and controversial required "Germany to accept the responsibility of Germany and her allies for causing all the loss and damage" during the war (the other members of the Central Powers signed treaties containing similar articles). This article, **Article 231**, later became known as the War Guilt clause. The treaty forced Germany to disarm, make substantial territorial concessions, and pay **reparations** to certain countries that had formed the Entente powers.

In 1921 the total cost of these reparations was assessed at 132 billion Marks (then $31.4 billion or £6.6 billion, roughly equivalent to US $442 billion or UK £284 billion in 2016). At the time economists, notably John Maynard Keynes, predicted that the treaty was too harsh – a "**Carthaginian peace**".
A part of Germany was handed over to France. Another part was given away to Belgium and Denmark. The important port of Danzig was taken by Poland. The "peace treaty" prohibited Germany from ever producing war planes and the German Army had to be under 100,000 soldiers, at all times in the future.

The economy of Germany was destroyed. The German government had no choice but to accept these insulting conditions. The common man was shattered at the sight of the nation's pride being molested. Inflation skyrocketed. Germans resorted to the ancient barter system for survival. Elderly couples across Germany started committing suicide by holding each other's hands and inhaling gas from the kitchen stove!

As conditions became dire, several groups of private citizens began openly defying the German government bound by the Treaty. Inflation had hit everyone equally: the rich as well as the poor. The right-wing capitalists and the left-wing workers came together to form a movement against the German government. The Army rose in revolt against the treaty in the Bavarian region. The main city in Bavaria – Munich – was put under siege.

Rebels started assassinating government officials. Those who actually signed the Treaty were taken out first. Many killings followed including those of ministers in the puppet government.

To make matters worse, German government failed to pay its debts. France, showing extreme ruthlessness, attacked a weak germany, swallowing Ruhr, a prosperous region in the German north-west. The region was the industrial heartland for raw materials. As a result, most of the German industry was shut down. 80% of the German working class became jobless.

It was time for someone to rise to the occasion and catch the falling nation. It was time for a leader to appear on the scene and change the course of history. The misfortune of his motherland and the plight of his fellow countrymen was making him restless. He vowed to fight for restoring Germany's glory. Revenge was on his mind. And Jews were the convenient soft target to vent his anger on. A failed painter. A defeated soldier. A wounded patriot. It was time for Adolf Hitler to make his move...

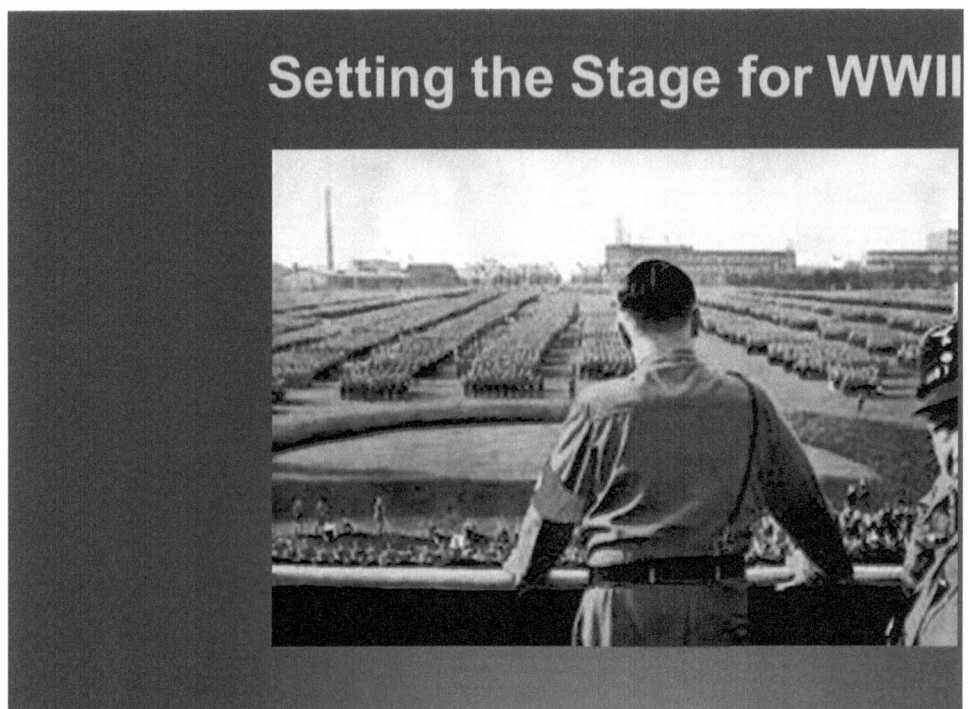

Pic courtesy: Slideplayer.

Rise of the Fury.

Using the Christian faith to justify his torture of Jews, Hitler planted a stereotype in the minds of the German public. An image of the mythical "wicked Jew". To help him gather public sympathy, war-hungry Allied Powers comprising of Great Britain and France showed no restraint in dealing with Germany post-WWI. Hitler rose to power on the back of a promise to make Germany great again.

Hitler had a disdain for communism. But Stalin up north in Russia was very much impressed by Hitler. The two would later forge a short-lived alliance.

As Germany suffered under the Treaty of Versailles as **Weimar Republic,** on October 29

1922, **Fascist** leader **Benito Mussolini** is appointed prime minister of Italy by king **Victor Emmanuel III** after the **March on Rome.** On November 1 in the same year, The **Grand National Assembly of Turkey** abolished the Ottoman Sultanate.

Turkey officially becomes a Republic following the dissolution of the **Ottoman Empire** on October 29, 1923.

On November 8, 1923, The **Beer Hall Putsch** takes place, in which **Adolf Hitler** unsuccessfully leads the Nazis in an attempt to overthrow the German government. It is crushed by police the next day.

Pic courtesy: Wikipedia.

On April 1, 1924, Adolf Hitler is sentenced to 5 years in jail for his participation in the Beer Hall Putsch. It is in jail where Hitler writes his autobiographical manifesto <u>Mein Kampf</u>.

In this manifesto, he clearly and in no uncertain terms chalks out the intent and the purpose of the Nazis. The work is filled with hatred for the Jews. Evoking religious mythology, Hitler justifies the belief that the Jews are an inferior race. It is extraordinarily similar to the kind of religious zealotry displaced by Islamists around world, justifying their cruel acts with holy scriptures.

Beginning in 1932, using shrewd political maneuvers, Hitler is invited to form a new government along with Paul von Hindenburg, President of Germany. **And on 30 January, 1933, Nazi leader Adolf Hitler is appointed Chancellor of Germany by President Paul von Hindenburg.**

Just few months after the coronation, German Parliament is set on fire. The **Reichstag Fire Decree** is passed, nullifying many German civil liberties, issued by **German President Paul von Hindenburg** on the advice of **Chancellor Adolf Hitler** in direct response to the **Reichstag fire** of 27 February 1933. Was the fire set purposefully by the Nazis for the excuse of suspending civil liberties?!!

As the United States elects FDR as their President, Hitler completes building the first concentration camp for the Jews. These camps would resemble public gardens from the outside, with music playing around them to calm the victims. Once inside the Jews would be subjected to poisonous gas which would make them vomit blood. Mass murder on steroids!

Courtesy: LIFE Images, Photo credit: Margaret Bourke-White.

On May 2, 1933, Hitler outlawed trade unions. Next month, all non-Nazi parties are banned in Germany. The same year in October, scientist Albert Einstein arrives in the United States as a refugee from Germany. The same month, Germany leaves the League of Nations.

The *Schutzstaffel or SS,* becomes an organization independent of the Nazi Party, reporting directly to **Adolf Hitler** on July 20, 1934. The same year, Japan renounces the Washington Naval Treaty and the London Naval Treaty.

Its amply clear where the world was headed. Just as we experience polarization in the world today, the Second World War was also preceded by deep and rapid polarization.

As Germany remilitarized the Rhineland, in defiance to the Treaty of Versailles, Italian troops march into Ethiopia. Amid chaos and confusion, Germany hosts the **1936 Summer Olympics** in **Berlin**.

The same year, German **Condor Legion** goes into action for the first time in the Spanish Civil War in support of the Nationalist side. Hitler was growing ambitious, fighting wars and taking sides far away from his Fatherland. As the year ended, Hitler made it mandatory for all males ages between 10-18 to join the Hitler Youth program.

Thousands of miles away, two opposing sides in the Chinese Civil War suspend hostilities to fight the common foe, Imperial Japan.

Mussolini sends 3,000 men of the Italian expeditionary force in support of the Nationalist side in the Spanish Civil War. Hitler's men fight alongside the Italian fascist for the first time. On Dec 11, 1937, Italy leaves the League of Nations. Just as Nazi Germany did 4 years ago…

Pic courtesy: Getty Images.

On March 15, 1939, Nazi Germany occupies Czechoslovakia. The Czechs do not attempt to put up any organized resistance having lost their main defensive line with the annexation of the Sudetenland.

Five days later, the German Foreign Minister **Joachim von Ribbentrop** delivers **an oral ultimatum to Lithuania,** demanding that it cede the **Klaipėda Region** (German name Memel) to Germany.

Next day, **Adolf Hitler** demands the return of the **Free City of Danzig** it lost to Poland because of the peace treaty. As Poland refuses, Hitler starts preparing for an invasion.

US President, sends a second letter to Hitler seeking peace. Hitler throws it in the dust-bin without even reading. On September 1, 1939, less than 24 hours after the German ultimatum to Poland had expired, Nazis invade Poland. The Second World War officially starts.

Pic courtesy: Archiwum Akt Nowych/Hugo Jaeger.

As Adolf Hitler salutes parading troops of the German Wehrmacht in Warsaw, Poland, on October 5, 1939 after the German invasion, the British government declared general mobilization of the British Armed Forces and starts evacuation plans in preparation of German air attacks.

Nazi Germany manages to cause great devastation in France as the nation is forced to surrender in shame. As panic sets in, the liberal Chamberlain government in Great britain falls. What replaces it is the administration of the bold, shrewd, unconventional and fierce leader Winston Churchill. Hitler had found his match!

December 7, 1941. The attack on Pearl Harbor leads to the United States' entry into World War II. Japan intended the attack as a preventive action to keep the U.S. Pacific Fleet from interfering with military actions they planned in Southeast Asia against overseas territories of the United Kingdom, the Netherlands, and the United States. What they did not count was the US response.

The attack commenced at 7:48 a.m. Hawaiian Time. The base was attacked by 353 Imperial Japanese fighter planes, bombers, and torpedo planes in two waves, launched from six aircraft carriers. All eight U.S. Navy battleships were damaged, with four sunk. **2,403 Americans were killed and 1,178 others were wounded.** Japanese losses were light: 29 aircraft and five midget submarines lost, and 64 servicemen killed. One Japanese sailor was captured.

AP Photo, U.S. Navy

The following day, December 8, the United States declared war on

Japan.

Subsequent operations by the U.S. prompted **Germany** and Italy to **declare war on** the U.S. on December 11, which was reciprocated by the U.S. the same day.

In the final year of the war, the **Allies** prepared for invasion of the **Japanese mainland**. This was preceded by a U.S. conventional and firebombing campaign that destroyed 67 Japanese cities. The war in Europe had concluded when Nazi Germany signed its instrument of surrender on May 8, 1945, just after Hitler committed suicide. The Japanese, facing the same fate, refused to accept the Allies' demands for **unconditional surrender** and the **Pacific War** continued.

The Allies called for the unconditional surrender of the **Japanese armed forces** in the **Potsdam Declaration** on July 26, 1945—the alternative being "prompt and utter destruction". The Japanese ignored it.

United States concluded that the invasion of Japanese homeland would prove to be very costly. Costs included financial as well as human. Hence it was decided that if Japan does not want to surrender, there was a need to end this war "quickly". The "Humanitarian value of Ruthlessness" was evoked.

On **August 6 1945**, the U.S. dropped a **uranium gun-type** (Little Boy) bomb on Hiroshima, and American President Harry S. Truman called for Japan's surrender, warning it to "expect a rain of ruin from the air, the like of which has never been seen on this earth." Three days later, **on August 9**, a plutonium implosion-type (Fat Man) bomb was dropped on Nagasaki.

Courtesy: Personnel aboard Necessary Evil derivative work & Charles Levy.

Within the first two to four months of the bombings, the acute effects of the atomic bombings killed 90,000–146,000 people in Hiroshima and 39,000–80,000 in Nagasaki; roughly half of the deaths in each city occurred on the first day. During the following months, large numbers died from the effect of burns, radiation sickness, and other injuries, compounded by illness and malnutrition.

Japan announced its surrender to the Allies on August 15, six days after the bombing of Nagasaki, officially ending the Second World War.

Churchill stirs the free world to victory. Despite bombing London for days and killing countless innocent Jews, Hitler was defeated by the grand alliance of two partners: Churchill and the United States.

Germany was divided. Berlin was partitioned with a wall. The world got its two new "superpowers". The United States and the Soviet Union. And the end of World War 2 was followed by the start of the Cold War. There was unfinished business to be done. The Trilogy started with the insignificant event of an Austrian archduke's assassination was yet to be completed. New evil forces were yet to raise their ugly head and new ideologies were yet to take birth. Freedom was not secure. Liberty was still at risk. And humanity had to face the horror of wars for many more decades, even a whole century!

India gained independence from the British, partly because a destroyed British economy due to war could not support colonial expeditions. The sun no longer shined bright on the British Empire. The British pound ceased to be the world's reserve currency. And the **Bretton Woods system** of monetary management was established. The United States now had just one superpower to compete with: The Soviet Union. As we would see, these two superpowers fought an indirect war with each other, while piling up dead bodies all over the world. The Great Game begins…

Pic courtesy below: Diercke International Atlas.

SECTION II

Chapter 2: Two Superpowers, One World.
When elephants dance, the earth shakes...

Pic courtesy: MASUDA JLLIMU

What was the Cold War? A 20th century confrontation between the Soviet Union and the United States, which spread from Europe to Asia, Africa, and Latin America, eventually dividing the world into two camps.

From Eastern Europe to the Middle East, every country is the world had to take sides. Even the newly independent nations were forced to be part of one camp or another. Depending on the decision, there were "consequences". For example, India, which was freed from the British rule in 1947 chose to be closer to the Soviet Union. The United States, consequently, befriended Pakistan to keep a check on the Soviet ally.

The series of one-upmanship between the US and the Soviet Republic entered the field of science and technology as well. From the latest war machines to space technology, these two giants competed in every field as if there was a war between them.

One of the direct consequences of this American fight against Communism as an ideology, was the Vietnam War.

Pic courtesy: Doan Cong Tinh/Patrick Chauvel Foundation

From 1 November 1955 to the **fall of Saigon** on 30 April 1975, it was a proxy war between North Vietnam and South Vietnam. The North was supported by the Soviets, the Chinese and other communist allies, while the South was aided by the Americans.

An adversary so much less capacity than the Americans was winning. And winning convincingly. After the Vietnam War drew to a close owing to large scale protests across America, driven partly by the large number of casualties suffered by the American forces, Communist governments took power in **South Vietnam**, **Laos** and **Cambodia**.
Complete withdrawal of **American-led forces** from **Indochina** occurred and North Vietnam annexed the Southern part of the region. Soviets won. Communism survived.

This lesson, that a weaker force on paper, can and does defeat a stronger force on the ground, led by guerrilla warfare and bravado, driven by ideological zealotry, was exactly what the Americans applied in Afghanistan when Soviets invaded.

Soviets showed great audacity and stationed nuclear missiles in Cuba. Enemy weapons so close to the homeland jolted the Americans, who in turn stepped up their campaign to bring the cold war closer to the Russian homeland.

Phoenix Weather

THE ARIZONA REPUBLIC

Today's Chuckle

THE STATE'S GREATEST NEWSPAPER

73rd Year, No. 57.   40 Pages   Phoenix, Arizona, Tuesday, October 23, 1962   TELEPHONE 27430   10¢   •   Tax Cents

U.S. BLOCKADES CUBA,
TELLS RUSS 'LAY OFF'

Will Sink Ships That Won't Halt

President's Cuba Stand Far-Reaching

Southeast Gears To War Pace

PRESIDENTIAL CLOSEUP

President Acts

Island's A-Missile Build-Up Cited

U.S. Acts To Back Speech

Image Credit: The Arizona State Library, Archives and Public Records

Cuban leader Fidel Castro was a strong Russian ally, along with his brother Raul Castro and the famous T-shirt figure Ernesto "Che" Guevara. Despite attempts to assassinate him more than 50 times, the CIA was unsuccessful. The map below shows the full range of Soviet missiles stationed in Cuba, used during the secret meetings on the Cuban crisis.

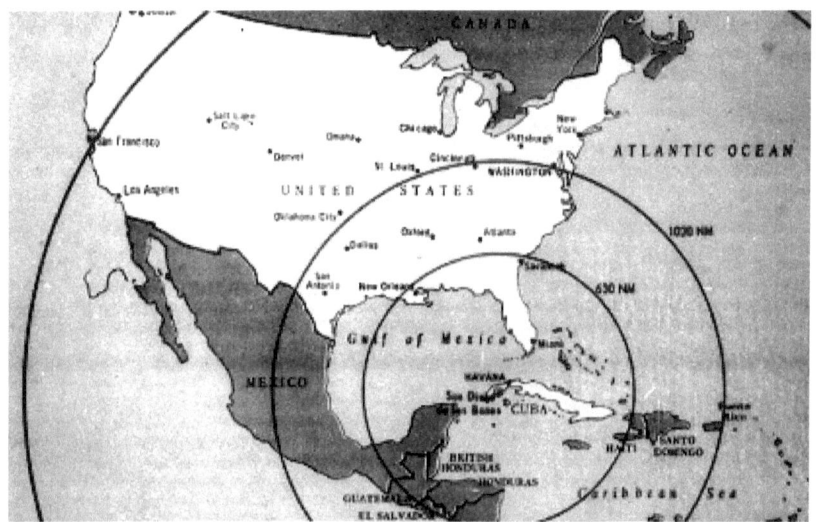
Pic courtesy: The John F. Kennedy Presidential Library and Museum

Americans meticulously developed deep assets inside the fringe states of the Soviet Union. Most of these states were ethnically different than Russians. Also they all practiced Islam. A clear point of differentiation existed. Using covert tactics, America successfully brought about the relatively peaceful disintegration of the Soviet Union.

Although what really delivered a big blow to the Soviet Union was its misadventure in Afghanistan. Desperate to secure oil in the resource rich regions of the Middle East, Soviets foolishly invaded Afghanistan. A nation known to be hostile to foreign invaders since the time of Alexander the Great.

April 27, 1978. Kabul. On this day, Afghan President Muhammad Daoud Khan, his family and supporters were brutally murdered, and the People's Democratic Party of Afghanistan took power. On December 27 1979, exactly 20 months later, Soviet Special Forces arrived in Afghanistan, under the garb of providing protection for Afghan President Hafizullah Amin. The Special Forces, however, stormed Amin's palace, killed him and engaged in a gory battle with the Afghan partisans that would drag on for more than nine years.

Pic courtesy; (AFP Photo / Vitaly Armand) / AFP

Mysterious capturing and killing of United States Ambassador
Adolph Dubs followed. United States taken aback by this Soviet
invasion quickly gathered local Afghan warlords to train and fight
the Russians. The man to lead this resistance was none other than
Osama Bin Laden, the son of a wealthy Saudi billionaire, exiled
from his home country for threatening its royal family.

Pic courtesy: The People's History.

Seen here is a triumphant Osama embolden by the fact that his ragtag army of local ill-equipped warriors had succeed in defeating a giant nuclear armed superpower with infinitely more resources to muster. Soviet defeat in Afghanistan paved the way for the American Century. A phase in which there was only one undisputed superpower. Only one standard: The American Standard. Only one consensus: The Washington Consensus. And only one reserve currency: The Might Dollar. American Exceptionalism was born…

Chapter 3: The American Century.
Almighty dollar reigns supreme...

In 1944 in Bretton Woods, New Hampshire, representatives from 44 nations met to develop a new international monetary system that came to be known as the **Bretton Woods system**. Members hoping the new system would "ensure exchange rate stability, prevent competitive devaluations, and promote economic growth." decided to settle their international accounts in dollars that could be converted to gold at a fixed exchange rate of $35 per ounce. It was not until 1958 that the Bretton Woods System became fully operational. Thus, the United States was committed to backing every dollar overseas with gold. Other currencies were fixed to the dollar, and the dollar was pegged to gold.

For the first few decades this new system worked very well. With the **Marshall Plan** in force, Japan and Europe were rebuilding themselves after the war, and countries outside the US wanted dollars to spend on American goods — cars, steel, machinery, etc. Because the U.S. owned over half the world's official gold reserves — 574 million ounces at the end of World War II — the system appeared secure.

A negative **balance of payments**, growing **public debt** incurred by the **Vietnam War**, and **monetary inflation** by the Federal Reserve caused the dollar to become increasingly overvalued in the 1960s.

In May 1971, **West Germany** left the Bretton Woods system, unwilling to revalue the **Deutsche Mark**. The dollar dropped 7.5% against the Deutsche Mark. Other nations began to demand redemption of their dollars for gold. **Switzerland** redeemed $50 million in July. France acquired $191 million in gold. On August 5, 1971, the **United States Congress** released a report recommending devaluation of the dollar, in an effort to protect the dollar against foreigners. On August 9, 1971, as the dollar dropped in value against European currencies, Switzerland left the Bretton Woods system. The pressure began to intensify on the United States to leave Bretton Woods.

Nixon Shock.

On August 15, 1971, President Nixon suspended the convertibility of the dollar into gold or other reserve assets, ordering the gold window to be closed such that foreign governments could no longer exchange their dollars for gold.

"Well, I don't give a shit about the lira…."

Nixon uttered these words while discussing the repercussions of going away from the Gold Standard. It is a shining example of the kind of arrogance that the world would see coming from the American side in matters of finance and monetary policy going forward. It continues to this day.

A year later the Bretton Woods system would fall apart as the US went off the gold standard altogether.

"Quote "
'I believe that banking institutions are more dangerous to our liberties than standing armies. If the American people ever allow private banks to control the issue of their currency, first by inflation, then by deflation, the banks and corporations that will grow up around the banks will deprive the people of all property until their children wake-up homeless on the continent their fathers conquered.'
Thomas Jefferson 1802

Pic courtesy: quoteaddicts.com

What the real consequences of this move would be, not just on foreign governments and the rest of the world; but also on the American people, would make itself clear only decades later, in the form of the 2008 financial crisis.

And the reason why it took so long for the ill-effects to express themselves in the real economy was the constant recycling of dollars through the global economy. A phenomenon popularly known as **Globalization**.

It is the same phenomenon Mr. Trump would run against, securing for himself the Presidency of the United States. It would be the same trend that would make China, once an American adversary in the Vietnam War, its biggest creditor. The holder of the largest US Treasury bills, a financial weapon China would not hesitate in using in the coming trade wars.

What this pivotal move by President Nixon actually did in the short term, was massive debt-fueled growth in the US economy. New capital was created out of thin air. Distributed across the economy fueling asset bubbles. It felt so good to be an American. The American Century had arrived, and people were lovin' it.

Nixon presented himself as a protector of the dollar, a warrior against inflation, and a jobs creator. That was his sales pitch. In the long run, this Tricky Dick (as he was known in politics) did the exact opposite. He set the stage for a large scale institutionalized addiction to "monetary heroin". A term that refers to the use of printing money by central banks to stimulate the economy. Also known as Quantitative Easing or QE, it is basically a massive price falsification operation, sanctioned by the government to punish savers in the economy.

The balance of payments swung from a persistent surplus to a chronic deficit.

United States: Current Account Balance % GDP (1960–2011)

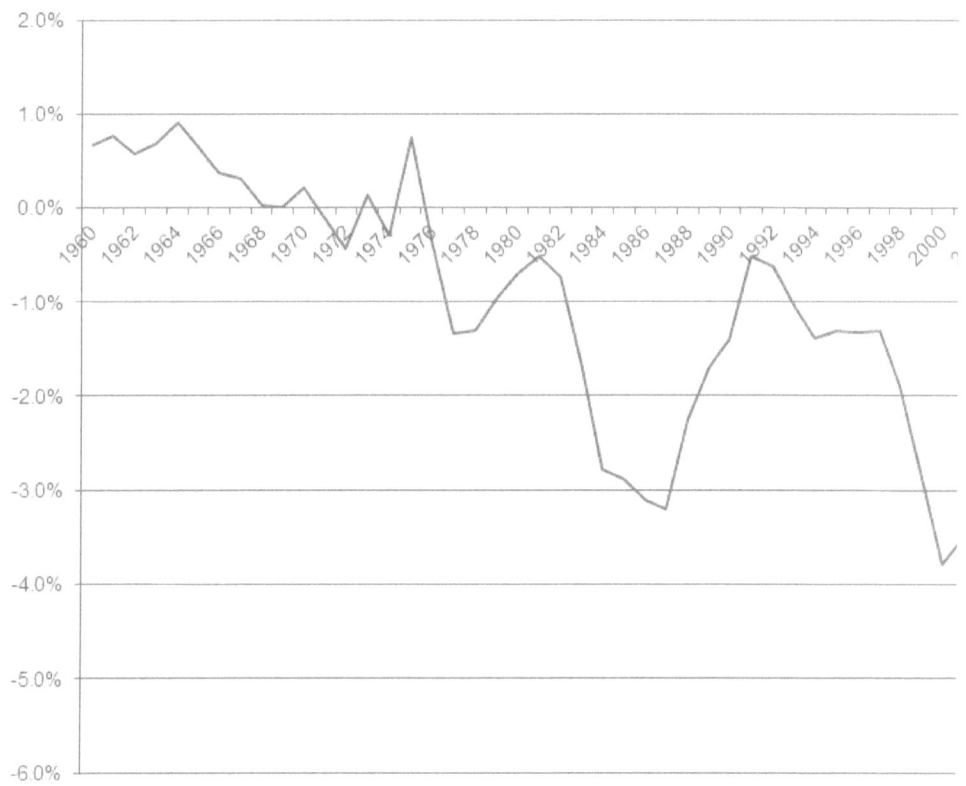

Sources: St. Louis Federal Reserve, CFA Institute.

United States started accumulating deficits, and throughout the Presidencies of Reagan and others who followed, this became a constant feature of the US economy. Interesting to note here; this character in the drama named Donald Trump was protesting against deficits even then. He had taken out big advertisements against even President Reagan for going soft on Japanese protectionism.

While the Almighty Dollar benefited the elites, goosed up financial assets and created huge fortunes for the few, American middle class was being systematically destroyed by US trade policies, undercutting American workers. The single largest drop in poverty in human history occurred in China, a direct result of Globalization.

Riding on cheap labour, China captured world markets, joined the World trade Organization (WTO) and surpassed Japan as an industrial nation. While America accumulated deficits, China enjoyed surplus. The wholesale destruction of American manufacturing ensued.

Had Bretton Woods remained intact, these events would not have happened. Under a gold standard, trade deficit countries (such as the United States today) pay trade surplus countries in gold to compensate them for the exchange of goods. This is the balancing mechanism of a gold standard, and it prevents countries from misallocating capital.

Almighty Dollar also made the US government irresponsible. Huge amount of debt, to fund social programs, was issued every year. With excess capital searching for a parking space, the bond markets got distorted. The only thing that keeps a government honest, a genuine bond market , was the last nail in sound money's coffin. The stage was set for the next Depression. And it came in the summer of 2008.

Meanwhile, other threats to the US economy remained. Most urgent was the threat of Islamic terrorism. A victorious Osama Bin Laden, turbocharged by his decisive triumph against the mighty Soviets, decided to turn the tables on the US.

SECTION III

Chapter 4: The Kingdom of Terror Crowns a New King.
   American fortress breached...

Source: ASKET

October 12, 2000. United States Navy guided-missile destroyer
USS *Cole* (DDG-67) was bombed while it was being refueled in
Yemen's Aden harbor. The terror attack was immediately linked to a
man America had helped train against the Soviets. Osama Bin
Laden. 17 U.S. sailors dead and another 39 injured.

Just a year ago, Bin Laden had appeared on the list of FBI's most wanted international criminals and terrorists. Actually Bin Laden developed bad blood with the Americans after the Iraqi invasion of Kuwait when US troops landed in Saudi Arabia. He was outraged by the presence of infidel forces so close to the Islamic holy sites of Mecca and Medina. Saudi government expels Laden who takes refuge in Sudan.

In December 1992, US troops land in Somalia for humanitarian work. Laden sends some of his trained fighters in the country to expel Americans. Two months later, a bomb explodes at the World Trade Center in New York City, bringing the fight between America and Bin Laden on US soil.

Pic courtesy: Federal Bureau of Investigation (FBI) website

6 killed. Hundreds wounded.

A month later, 18 U.S. servicemen, all of them part of a humanitarian mission to Somalia, are killed in an ambush in

Mogadishu. Bin Laden later says that some Arab Afghans were involved in the killings and calls Americans "paper tigers" because they withdrew from Somalia shortly after the soldiers' deaths.

In 1994, Saudi government officially strips Bin Laden off his citizenship, freezing all his assets in the country. His family disowns him immediately. CIA tries to kill him in an assassination attempt, but fails.

The target on the back of Americans in the Middle east continues with 5 more US troops killed in a truck bombing in a Riyadh military complex. 19 more US soldiers die in June 1996 in a Saudi military base.

On August 23, 1996, Osama Bin Laden officially declares a "holy war" on America. In his first interview to the Western media in 1997 to CNN, Bin Laden tells Peter Bergen that the United States is "unjust, criminal and tyrannical." "The U.S. today, as a result of the arrogant atmosphere, has set a double standard, calling whoever goes against its injustice a terrorist," he said in the interview. "It wants to occupy our countries, steal our resources, impose on us agents to rule us, and then wants us to agree to all this. If we refuse to do so, it says we are terrorists."

In February 1997, Bin Laden orders the militarization of the East African cell of Al Qaeda, a move that culminated in the bombing of the U.S. embassies in Kenya and Tanzania on August 7, 1998.

On August 7 1998, A pair of truck bombs explodes outside the U.S. embassies in Nairobi, Kenya, and Dar es Salaam, Tanzania. **Some 224 people are killed.**

Pic courtesy: Guardian Liberty Voice

The Day the World Changed Forever.

What is clear is Osama was growing increasingly bold in targeting America, at home and abroad. At least a couple of daily intelligence briefings to President Bush explicitly mentioned the threat of Bin Laden striking at home. One of those warnings even mentioned the use of commercial airplanes in the attack!

An interesting point to note here is that someone, very well connected to the terrorists and their plans, was trying to make a lot of money by betting on the US stock market to fall on the morning of 9/11. The stocks of the two airliners used in the attack painted a particularly interesting picture. As many traders in London and Hong Kong observed, massive shorts entered the market just after opening and even some orders came overnight, to sell. Did someone front-run the event? In that case, this particular group made a lot of money.

Profiting from a loss

The stocks of United and American airlines fell sharply following t
Sept. 11 terrorist attacks, which used hijacked jets from the two
But unknown investors made a bundle using a financial derivative
increases in value when a stock goes down.

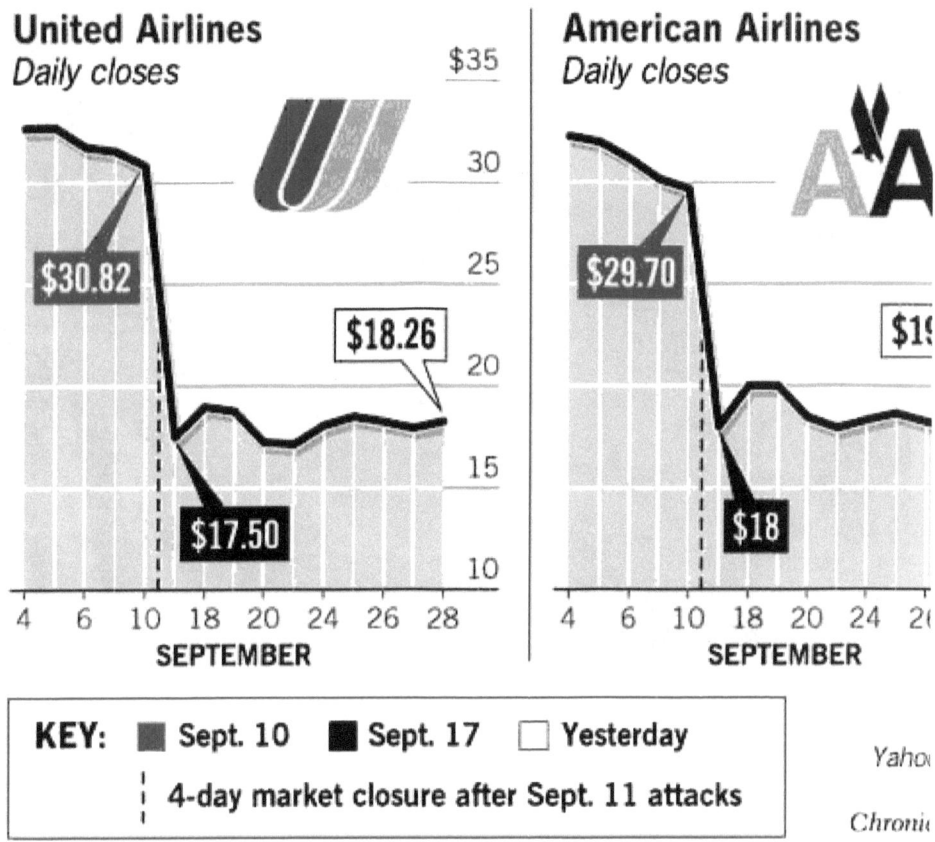

United Airlines
Daily closes

$35
30
25
20
15
10

$30.82
$18.26
$17.50

4 6 10 18 20 24 26 28
SEPTEMBER

American Airlines
Daily closes

$29.70
$1!
$18

4 6 10 18 20 24 2(
SEPTEMBER

KEY: ■ Sept. 10 ■ Sept. 17 ☐ Yesterday

4-day market closure after Sept. 11 attacks

Yaho\
Chroni\

Just months after experiencing the dot-com burst, again, a direct
consequence of the flawed monetary policies we analysed in the
previous chapter, the US markets were once more subjected to
mayhem and chaos. Add to the tragedy the massive loss of human
life in the terror attacks, the likes of which America had never seen

in her 200+ years of existence!

Pic courtesy: Getty Images.

President Bush declared to the world: "Every nation, in every region, now has a decision to make. Either you are with us, or you are with the terrorists."

America which turned a blind eye to the threat of Islamic terrorism, which was causing great harm to other democracies especially India, the same monster it nurtured for geopolitical gain, was now attacking the host. It is important to remember at this point that India was suffering from Islamic terrorism since Pakistan, a failed state, started diverting Jihadis from Afghanistan, where they were no longer needed to fight the Russian, to Kashmir.

Pakistani dictator Muhammad Zia-ul-Haq actively supported these mujahideens against India. The concept of "good terrorist and bad terrorist" was born. Interestingly, Al-Qaeda, the name of Bin Laden's criminal organisation is actually a book, written by the man himself. Its preface was written by this Pakistani thug in military uniform, Zia-ul-Haq.

The Invasion of Afghanistan & Iraq.

The Taliban government in Afghanistan led by Mullah Omar was thought to be giving shelter to the most wanted man on earth, Bin Laden. But as America would discover later, it was Pakistan which provided, not just a place to live, but also crucial medical aid to Osama after 9/11. The man went on dialysis a few years after 9/11. He always cherished the dream to see America fall in his lifetime. To fulfill his goal, he often met Pakistani nuclear scientists and Afghan officials immediately after attacking the American homeland. The purpose was thought to be mining for Uranium in Afghanistan. Obviously to make a dirty bomb.

This, experts believe, was the real reason why President Bush invaded Afghanistan. US knew even after toppling the Taliban government in Kabul, 9/11 masterminds would escape. Primary aim was to thwart Bin Laden's plan to get hold of uranium reserves in Afghanistan. The arrest of Abu Zubaid in Pakistan made it clearly this was exactly what Laden was after.

It was around the same time Saddam Hussein was establishing close contacts with Al-Qaeda. Certain factions within the group, who were fiercely against Saddam were thrown out of Al-Qaeda. Iraq wanted to develop WMDs (Weapons of Mass Destruction) using the Uranium reserves Osama was seeking. Pakistan played the part of a broker, to perfection.

Initial trials of WMDs were successful on dogs and prisoners in Iraq. And the man behind the trials was not Saddam. It was Abu Musab Al Zarqawi. A terrorist 10 times more ruthless than Osama, who Zarqawi openly considered "mild".

What followed next was unexpected. Zarqawi was unceremoniously removed from Al-Qaeda citing his anti-Shia rhetoric. He formed a terror group of his own called Jund al-Sham, in Syria. Zarqawi was supposedly killed by US airstrikes. Note that this is the a similar sounding outfit which has publicly claimed responsibility for killing the Russian ambassador in Turkey! So is Zarqawi still alive? Is his terror group still operational in Syria? Only time will tell…

Chapter 5: The House of Cards Collapses.
When money grew on trees…

The 2008 financial crisis was the worst economic disaster since the Great Depression of 1929. It led to the Great Recession. where housing prices fell more than 32%, worse than the 1929 Depression. Two years after the recession, unemployment was still above 9%, and discounting the discouraged workers who had given up search for work. They were no longer counted as unemployed.

It started when housing prices started to drop in 2006. Realtors were relieved. They thought the overheated housing market was cooling off. What realtors didn't realize was the number of homeowners with no income, who had taken loans for 100% (or more) of their home's value. Predatory lending had millions of victims.

But why did banks lend to such consumers? What was in it for the financial institutions to handle such risk assets? Answer to this question is Greed. Of Course the banks want to make a profit. And profit earned through adding value advances the cause of economic prosperity. But what the banks were doing, and are still engaged in such practices is called the financial industry calls **Securitization**.

The original mortgages had been chopped up and resold in tranches, the actual derivatives resulting from this perverse practices were impossible to price. No one wanted to be caught holding the bag. Banks resisted lending to each other so they wouldn't get stuck with the potentially worthless mortgages as collateral. As a result, interbank borrowing costs also known as LIBOR, rose. Liquidity collapsed and the global economy was on the brink of bankruptcy.

In 2007, the Federal Reserve began pumping liquidity into the banking system. It wasn't enough. In March 2008, investors went after Bear Stearns, which was rumored to have way too many of these toxic assets. Bear Stearns approached JP Morgan Chase for a bail out. Instead, the situation deteriorated through the summer of 2008. The Treasury Department was authorized to spend up to $150 billion to subsidize and eventually take over Fannie Mae and Freddie Mac.

The public went into panic. Angry depositors were warned by Los Angeles police to remain calm while they waited in line to withdraw funds from a failed bank.

Too big to fail. The phrase was used during the 2008 financial crisis. It described why the government needed to bail out some companies. It is a stunning display of Corporatism. A cartel of big banks and big corporations lobbying the government to save their failed businesses. Such a nice treatment was not meted out to the ordinary people about to be thrown out of their own houses!

Interesting to note, Lehman Brothers was as important to the US and global economy as Bear Stearns. But it was allowed to fail. Reason being the investment bank had a lot of assets of US geopolitical adversaries. It's a shining example of how global finance and geopolitics is intertwined. This looks like a permanent feature in the ongoing Third World War. Business decisions influenced by politics, and international relations based on financial interests rather than values or principles.

Financialism, Not Capitalism.

This is not capitalism, full stop. John Adams once wrote, "The moment the idea is admitted into society, that property is not as sacred as the law of God, and that there is not a force of law and public justice to protect it, anarchy and tyranny commence." George Mason himself had declared, "Frequent interference with private property and contracts, retrospective laws destructive of all public faith, as well as confidence between man and man, and flagrant violations of the Constitution must disgust the best and wisest part of the community, occasion a general depravity of manners, bring the legislature into contempt, and finally produce anarchy and public convulsion."

It wasn't just the Founding Fathers of America who called private property the "bedrock of capitalism", though of course they never used those terms invented later, as it had been very well understood especially as an outgrowth of the Enlightenment.

Thirty-nine delegates signed the United States Constitution in September 1787, but three refused to. Throughout the country there was a great debate more so about what was missing from it.

The **Fifth Amendment** decrees, **"No person shall be…deprived of life, liberty, or property, without due process of law; nor shall private property be taken for public use, without just compensation."** Private property is central to this amendment because private property was understood then as a central check not just on government but as the primary tangible instrument of freedom. There was and is everything a man might think up and dream, but what he could do with such endeavors is as important in the plying of a just and stable social arrangement.

Rate Rank	State Name	NOD	LIS	NTS	NFS	REO	Total	1/every X HU (rate)	%
									Properties with Foreclosure Filings

Rate Rank	State Name	NOD	LIS	NTS	NFS	REO	Total	1/every X HU (rate)
--	U.S.	57,031	58,171	108,875	32,622	79,474	336,173	380
24	Alabama	0	0	1,966	0	750	2,716	787
36	Alaska	0	0	165	0	45	210	1,344
3	Arizona	12	0	11,263	0	5,559	16,834	158
22	Arkansas	143	0	1,062	0	462	1,667	772
2	California	44,258	0	36,145	0	20,642	101,045	132
9	Colorado	6	0	4,004	0	1,714	5,724	372
46	Connecticut	0	56	0	115	56	227	6,337
29	Delaware	0	0	0	235	106	341	1,140
	District of Columbia	186	0	155	0	76	417	682
4	Florida	0	32,220	0	13,312	7,367	52,899	165
6	Georgia	1	0	11,050	0	2,973	14,024	282
19	Hawaii	155	0	460	0	91	706	718
8	Idaho	1,098	0	745	0	38	1,881	335
11	Illinois	0	3,648	0	3,998	3,150	10,796	486
13	Indiana	0	1,776	0	2,282	1,510	5,568	499
41	Iowa	0	0	266	0	294	560	2,374
33	Kansas	0	215	0	491	252	958	1,273
40	Kentucky	0	415	0	414	300	1,129	1,688
34	Louisiana	0	131	0	1,046	275	1,452	1,280
42	Maine	0	99	0	157	36	292	2,386
21	Maryland	0	2,251	0	246	603	3,100	748
26	Massachusetts	0	2,048	0	771	402	3,221	845
7	Michigan	0	0	7,965	0	5,642	13,607	333
18	Minnesota	7	0	1,736	0	1,589	3,332	692
39	Mississippi	0	0	441	0	314	755	1,662
27	Missouri	1	0	1,567	0	1,544	3,112	851
47	Montana	0	0	2	0	60	62	7,025
45	Nebraska	0	128	0	3	18	149	5,240
1	Nevada	8,726	0	6,252	0	3,786	18,764	59
37	New Hampshire	0	0	417	0	21	438	1,356
25	New Jersey	0	2,405	0	1,325	603	4,333	808
31	New Mexico	0	303	0	273	134	710	1,214
38	New York	0	3,614	0	756	480	4,850	1,637
35	North Carolina	767	0	1,184	0	1,224	3,175	1,299
49	North Dakota	0	0	0	19	13	32	9,705
10	Ohio	0	4,121	0	3,981	3,150	11,252	450
32	Oklahoma	445	0	532	0	318	1,295	1,253
14	Oregon	36	0	2,125	0	952	3,113	517
28	Pennsylvania	0	1,945	0	2,020	976	4,941	1,109
12	Rhode Island	0	0	30	0	882	912	494
30	South Carolina	0	996	0	214	476	1,686	1,199
44	South Dakota	0	81	0	30	2	113	3,161
15	Tennessee	0	0	2,782	0	1,893	4,675	583
23	Texas	13	0	7,668	0	4,342	12,023	785
5	Utah	1,170	0	1,571	0	730	3,471	267
50	Vermont	0	0	0	0	11	11	28,312
17	Virginia	7	0	3,531	0	1,650	5,188	631
16	Washington	0	0	3,642	0	1,036	4,678	587
48	West Virginia	0	0	101	0	13	114	7,743
20	Wisconsin	0	1,719	0	934	878	3,531	725
43	Wyoming	0	0	48	0	36	84	2,885

How did a giant insurance company become one of the largest bailouts in the 2008 financial crisis? To boost its balance sheet, AIG had become a major seller of "credit default swaps" (CDS).These swaps insured the assets that supported corporate debt and mortgages. If AIG went bankrupt, it would trigger the bankruptcy of many of the "too big to fail" financial institutions which bought these swaps.

AIG was so large that its demise would impact the entire global economy. For example, the $4 trillion money-market fund industry invested in AIG's debt and securities. Most mutual funds owned AIG stock. Financial institutions around the world were also major holders of AIG's debt.

After taking the bailout, AIG had the nerve to pay $165 million in bonuses to its executives, the same people who messed up. People were outraged, even issuing death threats against AIG CEO Edward Liddy.

Fiat currency, the source of boom-bust cycle.

Also called "Toilet Paper Money", the history of fiat money has been one of failure. In fact, every fiat currency since the Romans first began the practice in the 1st century has ended in devaluation and eventual collapse, of not only the currency, but of the economy that circulated this poison within it.

In recent times, fiat failures have become more common occurrences. In 1932, Argentina had the eighth largest economy in the world before its currency collapsed. In 1992, Finland, Italy, and Norway had currency shocks that spread through Europe.

In 1994, Mexico went through the infamous "Tequila Hangover".
In 1997, the Thai baht fell through the floor and the effects spread to
Malaysia, the Philippines, Indonesia, Hong Kong, and South Korea.
The Russian Ruble, Zimbabwe and more recently Argentina again
have clearly demonstrated the destructive power of fiat currency.

The U.S. has a debt similar to that of Weimar Germany. With the
dollar supply increasing (through printing more money by the fed) at
a rate of 13% per annum, this **overissuance** of a currency has been
the **leading indicator of a currency on the brink.**

Chapter 6: American Exceptionalism Challenged.
The eagle ages…

Belief in America and in her exceptionalism has become a fundamentalism religion. But does the "indispensable nation" really live up to the stature the world awards it? A cursory look will yield the answer: Yes, it does. Every other nation is relatively worse off than America. Americans also have the added advantage of geography. Both geopolitical and geological. While there are no sworn enemies sharing a border with America, she is blessed with enormous natural resources under the ground. From Shale oil & gas to coal and renewables. So what is America's Achilles heel?

In one word: **Debt**.

Debt works the same way for countries as it does for individuals and families: ***When you borrow too much your life spins out of control.*** For national and multinational entities that means elections become unpredictable, economies function erratically, and public policies become more ad hoc and less effective. **And civil unrest becomes the rule rather than the exception**.

As the US is getting bogged down by Debt, other countries, especially those who are American adversaries, are funding an opening to come at the US once again. The **Rise of Putin** as also the aggressive posturing by China is a direct consequence of American failure to project strength the way it used to.

Aging With Debt

Number of Americans whose Social Security checks were ga
due to unpaid federal student-loan debt

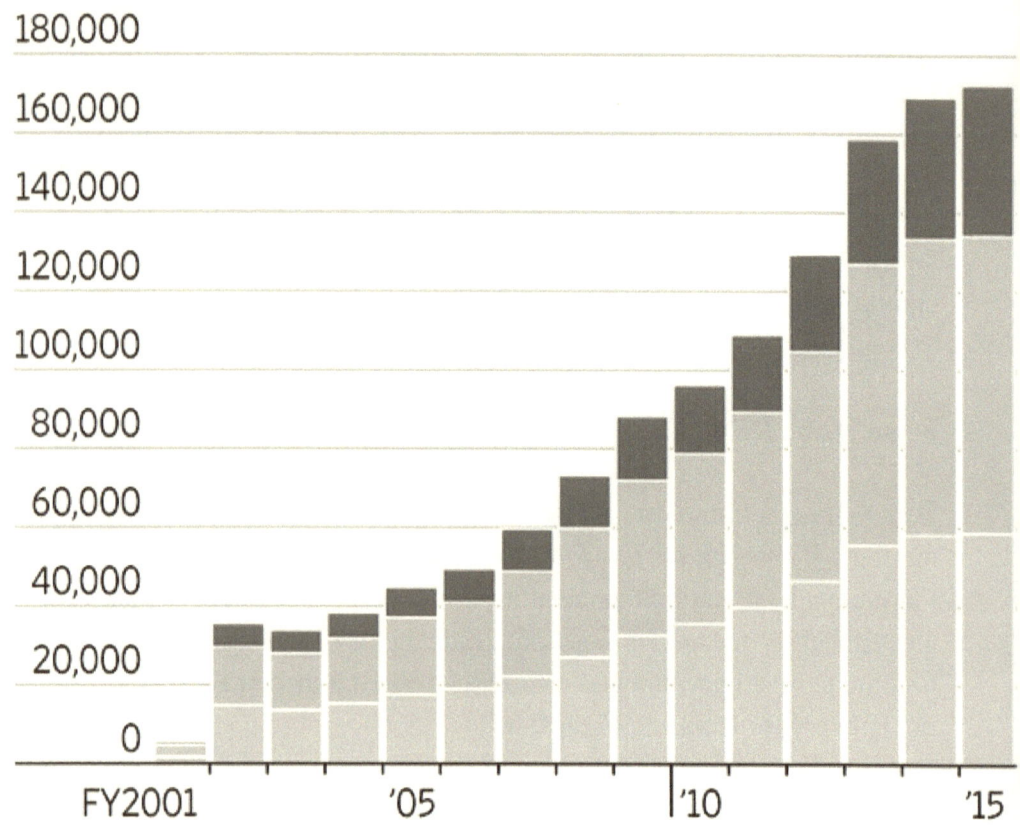

Note: Fiscal year ends Sept. 30.
Source: Government Accountability Office

THE WALL STRE

The alarming rise in the number shootings across the US, the
constant threat of the "debt ceiling" in Washington, and the
dangerous accumulation of US debt by China, which can be used as
a financial weapon in the event of a trade war (Trump has promised

it!), is a matter of serious concern for the US.

Mother Russia rises again.

Born in 1952, Vladimir Putin was a KGB agent responsible for managing the ex-Soviet nations that broke away from the Union in the 90s. All these nations are Islamic. Hence Putin's special hatred for Islamic terrorism. Russia is still not gotten over the fact that the Soviet Union is dead. Putin's grand scheme is to reconstruct Mother Russia, a region Russian patriots regard as the Russian motherland. It includes all of the former Soviet fringe states that broke away, and also some new states in Eastern Europe. The only obstacle in the way is NATO.

1st December 2013. Ukrainian police break up student protest camp in Kiev's Independence Square.

Courtesy: Reuters.

20th February 2014. More than 100 people reportedly die in 48 hours as protesters and police clash in Kiev, with government snipers opening fire.

22nd February 2014. Viktor Yanukovych, president of Ukraine, flees Kiev.

27th February 2014. Pro-Russian gunmen seize government buildings in Simferopol, the capital of Ukraine's Crimea peninsula.

12 November, 2014. NATO commander Gen Philip Breedlove reports Russian military equipment and Russian combat troops have been **seen entering Ukraine** in columns over several days.

Diplomats use the language to hide their thoughts, and the true position of a state is never spoken of openly (otherwise, there would not be any need to maintain the intelligence and counterintelligence agencies). We can only judge the true goals and intentions of a state by its actions.

Pic courtesy: Reuters.

Aleppo, Syria.

The theatre of indirect war between Russia and the US is now shifting to the Middle East. ISIS, a terror group infinitely more violent than Al-Qaeda has taking over massive territory fueled by stolen oil revenues. It is said that the US, Israel, Saudi Arabia and Turkey covertly help the Sunni ISIS, in order to use it against Shia Iran.

Iran on the other hand uses violent Shia militia to neutralize Saudi/Sunni interests in the region. As American grip on the middle east loosens, China is coming in with massive aid and trade. Saudi Arabia has openly declared China to be its most important customer for oil in the future, partly owing to the fear of the American Shale Oil revolution.

The result of all this is an intense fight between US and Russia in Syria. Bashar Assad, the Syrian dictator, is Shia. Traditional American allies in the region are all Sunni, including Pakistan. Russia, in a desperate move to gather some lost momentum in the region, is befriending the Shia powers, while American is holding on to its traditional Sunni allies. A SHia-Sunni theatre of war is unfolding at a rapid rate.

(AFP Photo/George Ourfalian)

It's a big mess. Add to the mix the only nuclear armed Muslim State in the world: Pakistan. Pakistan is a Sunni majority country, founded by a Shia. This dichotomy in its national character since the time of birth in 1947 has never left the psyche of Pakistan's ruling elite: Its military.

Daily clashes between various sects of Islam is a commonplace in the country. A nation that survives solely on opium trade coming from Afghanistan has to beg for constant military and civilian aid in front of anyone who is willing to extra the next pound of flesh from the failed state.

Result is a nation who has lost its reason for existence, Like an unstable chemical compound, Pakistan may break up at any point in time. America is well aware of this. That's why despite ample evidence to suggest that Pakistani Army plays a double game with the US troops in Afghanistan and the fact that Osama Bin Laden was found in the country, the US continues to provide financial aid. For the US knows, China is waiting to
fill that vacuum.

South China Sea. The Pacific Theatre.

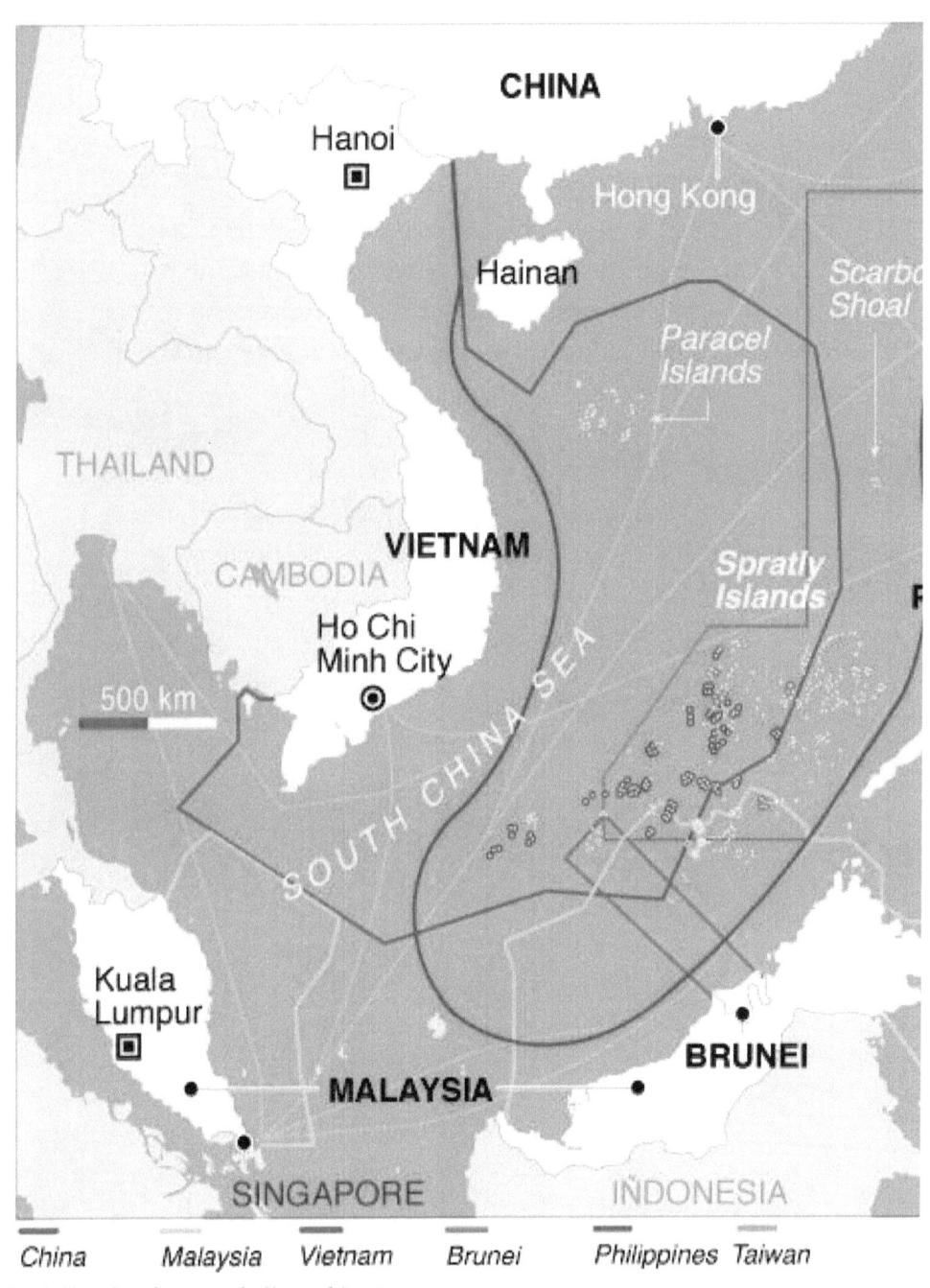

South China Sea claims map by Voice of America

When a known superpower is in decline, the wannabes start advancing. China's aggressive posturing in the international waters of the South China Sea is an example of this trend. Just as animals close in on a weak prey, hyenas gather around a weak lion cub or a wounded lion male.

The dispute is not limited to the US. China wants to target japan as well. It is also an attempt to test the willingness of the US to engage in fight abroad, especially after the debacles of Afghanistan & Iraq. **It may well be a trial balloon by China to test if they can swallow Taiwan!**

China now building a military complex on the disputed islands and installing nuclear weapons on it! A direct threat to not just Japan and US pacific assets but also to the smaller nations of Vietnam, Philippines and others.

Woody Island Overview, Feb. 17, 2016

Pic courtesy: Stratfor

What we can conclude from the various fronts developing in this drama called the Third World War, is that this will be the **first time America will have to fight a war on its own soil.**

Chapter 7: The Climax.
What will it be…

Going Forward.

As Islamic Jihad becomes increasingly more powerful, partly due to the Western world's political correctness and partly because the Jihadists grow more desperate, terrorists attacks across the democratic world are expected to rise exponentially.

Fuelled by Saudi Arabia, the Sunni terror groups may launch a direct attack on Shia Iran, shedding any pretense of diplomacy or restraint.

Remember that Saudi Arabia is finding in extremely tough to balance the budget due to low oil price. One way of boosting the oil price is by fuelling war in the region. In is estimated the Saudi Kingdom may go bankrupt by 2020. They need an oil price higher than $105 to break even on their oil production. Anything less is a deficit for the Kingdom.

One of the biggest enemies of Saudi oil, is US Shale. As the international crude price rises, it becomes more profitable to extract Shale in America. This has a dampening effect on oil price which in turn hurts Saudis. Shale innovates to stay profitable at lower and lower oil price but Saudis cant.

Iran on the other hand does not mind selling crude cheap just for the fun of hurting the Saudis. Biggest beneficiaries are oil importing countries like India & China. They get a great deal.

A Rose in the Desert.

A Jewish nation surrounded by Arab enemies, fighting for survival since formation. Israel has the distinction of defeating 6 Arab armies simultaneously while capturing additional territory in the process! In the ongoing WW3, Israel is playing a crucial role. On one hand Israel funds Sunnis terror groups like ISIS to counterbalance Shia fanaticism. On the other hand, the nation has a deep influence on American politics. The Israel Lobby in the US will play a pivotal role in the ever-changing equations in the middle east and beyond.

Interesting to note that while Russia is campaigning against ISIS, the very group Israel covertly buys oil from, Israel-Russia relations have never been better.

Fake Ottomans rise.

With the assassination of the Russian ambassador in Ankara, Turkey has openly crossed swords with the Russian bear. Putin will have his revenge. In the meantime, Turkey, a relatively moderate Muslim nation is turning radical at an alarming pace. Will Turkey be the gateway to Europe for Jihadis from Syria? Is the border between Turkey and Greece/Bulgaria be the new Gates of Vienna?

South of the Himalayas.

As the world's largest democracy, India will be central to the scenes unfolding. But since India does not have a working "foreign policy", neither does the country take sides in an international dispute, India will conserve its energies to fight at the end of the war. As the world's fastest growing nation, surpassing China, India can be of great help in the rehabilitation phase.

Mad Men of the East.

If there is one country that qualifies for the title of lunatics, it has to be North Korea. China uses the small nation as its pawn against Japan, and increasingly South Korea. In the coming years it is quite possible that China uses North Korea to wage a war with South Korea, a US ally. 20,000 US soldiers are stationed in South Korea. China does not like their presence so close to the homeland one bit.

Evil forces combine?

Is there a possibility of evil forces of China, North Korea, Pakistan and its Arab allies (whoever survives the Shia-Sunni grind!) coming together putting up a united front to fight democratic forces? Ofcourse!

Biological Warfare.

The intentional spread of germs, viruses and diseases to cause maximum with minimum risk can be termed as Biological warfare. Islamic terrorists have trying to get their hands on biological weapons for quite some time now. Their success is doomsday for the civilised world.

Chemical Warfare.

Use of poisonous gases on the frontlines was first used by the Allied powers against Germany in the first world war. Hitler copied the technique and used is against the same nations in the second world war. Not to forget his brutal and inhuman campaign against the Jews, driven by chemical warfare. Japan also used it against China during the second world war and earlier. Chemical weapons were recently used by Syrian dictator Assad against hi own people, those who supported the rebels. Its use is much more common during a war than say Biological weapons.

Space Warfare.

"Killing" the satellites of adversaries will increasingly be used. It will either be done from the ground using a space missiles, or other "killer satellites" may be deployed to take down enemy hardware orbiting in space. US has demonstrated the capacity many times, killing its own satellites to send a message to opponents. Laser beams capable of reducing targets on the ground to rubble are also being developed.

Cyber Wars.

DoS (Denial of Service) attacks that temporarily blacked out the whole Internet were witnessed by the entire world recently. Then there was China's attempt to steal American military secrets using cyber attacks on the Pentagon. Russia was also accused of meddling in the recently concluded US elections by hacking the servers of the Democratic party, a party much more opposed to friendly relations with Russia than the Republican Party. In the coming years the scale of such attacks will increase, with big corporations coming under back-breaking assaults. Information including financial, military, trade secrets, diplomatic materials etc are a legitimate target in this war.

Conclusion.

As President-elect Donald Trump continues to surprise the world with his new appointments in key positions, the world is certainly moving toward the completion of the Trilogy that started, remember, when an Austrian archduke was assassinated by Austrians of Slav origin, who had their loyalties with Serbia!

Trump's cabinet picks so far look like generals in this war against Islamic Jihad & China!
It also signals friendship with Russia.
1) State Secretary (Foreign Minister): An old Russian friend.
2) Defense Secretary (Defense Minister): Mad Dog Mattis, a Churchill style ruthless operator!
3) CIA Director: A fiercely anti-Muslim hawk!
4) Treasury Secretary (Finance Minister): A Goldman hand, who believes in using the fiat currency to achieve political goals.
5) National Security Adviser: Openly anti-Sharia, he has vowed to defeat Islamic Jihad at home and abroad.
6) Chief Strategist: A strong anti-immigration advocate.
7) Head of National Trade Council: An author of the book, "Death By China", he is as much anti-trade with China as anyone else. Trade wars are a given.

China Treasury Holdii

2008   2009   2010   2011   2012   2013   2014   2015

Pic courtesy: zerohedge.

Add to this the fact that the US government has just announced that they are putting Alibaba, a giant Chinese e-commerce company, on the list of websites selling fake merchandise.

Trump team is also proposing a 10% import tariff on all goods coming into the United States from China. The first shot in the trade war? We will find that out soon...

Geopolitics is coming a full circle. Russia which was an indirect ally of the United States in the second world war, is now once again looking at America and her new President with friendly eyes.

Obama legacy looks to be drowning as Trump has vowed to reverse Obama's every executive action. Blacks are once again feeling insecure in a country their elders fought to have equal rights.

Nationalism is on the rise in the West, once again!

Far Right parties are sweeping polls, from Australia to America to the heartland of Europe.

India has taken war on black money and corruption to a new level, hurting the Pakistani fake currency printing press industry. Also, the nuclear-armed country of over 1.2 billion people successfull tested a nuke-capacity missile named Agni-5 that can reach every city in China!

Meanwhile, Europe is suffering from terror attacks, either in the form of mass murder like the Berlin Christmas market truck crash or the frequent molestation of European women at the hands of refugees. If civil war breaks out in Europe, as feared by the French President, the situation will truly be of an explosive kind.

Latin American & African countries are especially vulnerable to currency failures first, as we are witnessing in Argentina. It will only aid China, which will capitalize on their misery; and Islamists who are busy setting up base in South America.

Let's keep our fingers crossed. And may Liberty triumph.